CHURCHES
CHARACTERS
&
COUNTRY WALKS

Liz Jones

combines all three along Devon's byways and footpaths

To Vicky & Bella
constant companions

First published in Great Britain in 1992

Copyright © Liz Jones, 1992

ORCHARD PUBLICATIONS
2 Orchard Close
Chudleigh
Newton Abbot
Devon TQ13 0LR
Tel: (0626) 852714

British Library Cataloguing in Publication Data
CIP Catalogue Record for this book is available from the British
Library
ISBN 0 9519027 3 3

Designed and typeset for Orchard Publications by
Bovey Tracey TeleCottage
Courtenay House
76 Fore Street
Bovey Tracey
Newton Abbot
Devon TQ13 9AD
Tel: (0626) 835757

Illustrations by Ann Brightmore-Armour

Printed by
Moor Print, Manaton, Devon

PREFACE

I find a walk more appealing if there is a point of special interest along the way. With this in mind the theme of these walks is the parish church. All the churches featured have people connected with them who are in some way notable. Some may be well-known, others not so famous, but I hope the reader will be inspired to undertake these rambles.

All walks are circular and of varying lengths to cater for all abilities. Some walks are demanding but details of the terrain are included to assist the reader in deciding if the walk is suitable. Times quoted allow a leisurely pace in order to visit the churches and enjoy the countryside.

As much information as possible about parking areas, refreshment stops and maps required has been given. Please remember to park considerately and, if walking with a dog keep it under control.

Maps used are :	Landranger	1:50.000 = 1" to 1 mile
	Outdoor Leisure	1:25.000 = 2" to 1 mile
	Pathfinder	1:25.000 = 2" to 1 mile

It is recommended that the moorland walks are only undertaken in good weather. A compass will be required for all walks, but only for general direction guidance, as opposed to strict route finding.

Comprehensive instructions for reading a grid reference will be found on the Landranger and Outdoor Leisure maps.

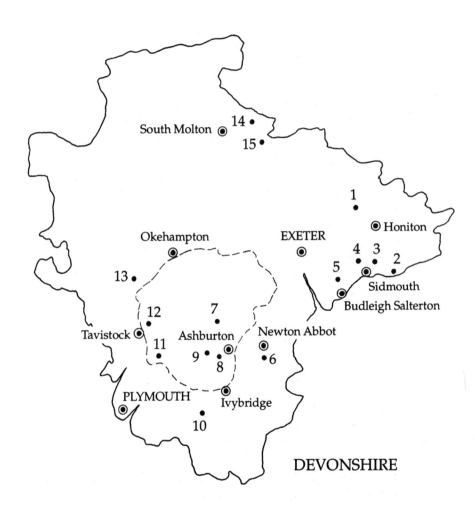

South Molton ◉ 14 •
                15 •

                            1 •

                                    ◉ Honiton

Okehampton   EXETER   4   3
        ◉   ◉   5 • • ◉ • 2 •
13 •   •
                                    Sidmouth
                        ◉
                   Budleigh Salterton

        12   7 •
Tavistock ◉ •   Ashburton   Newton Abbot
        11 •   ◉   ◉
           •   9 • •   • 6
                   8

PLYMOUTH   ◉
        ◉   Ivybridge
           10 •

                    DEVONSHIRE

INDEX

Reverend Toplady memorial

BROADHEMBURY - NORTH HILL

Distance:	Approx. 5½ miles
Time:	Allow 3 - 4 hours
Map:	OS Landranger 192; Pathfinder ST00/10
Start reference:	ST102048
Terrain:	Roads, bridleways and field paths
Nearest Town:	Honiton
Parking:	Near church
Refreshments:	Drewe Arms, Broadhembury
Church:	St. Andrew's, Broadhembury
Connection:	Revd. Augustus Toplady (1740 - 1778)*
	Author of Hymn *'Rock of Ages'*
	Vicar 1768 - 1778

It was whilst Vicar at Broadhembury that Toplady wrote the hymn *'Rock of Ages.'* In 1775 this hymn was published in the Gospel Magazine, apparently having been inspired by the time he sheltered from a storm in a cleft of limestone rock at Burrington Combe in the Mendips.

From the parking area, continue up the lane to the church with its impressive 100 foot tower. Much of the church dates from the 15th century, including the octagonal font bearing the figures of saints. The 500 year old painted wagon roof over the nave still retains much of its original colour. There are a number of memorials to be seen, particularly to the Drewe family, whose chapel was once the South Chancel. The memorial to Toplady is found in the Sanctuary, placed here 120 years after his death.

On leaving the church walk on through the churchyard to exit onto the minor road to Dunkeswell and Sheldon; bear right (NE)

St. Andrews - Broadhembury

along the road. A steady climb, offering views to the left, leads past Stafford Barton to Lane End Cross. Keep on the Dunkeswell road to ascend Stafford Hill. On a hot day, there is welcome shade from the overhanging trees along this road.

Almost at the hill's summit, where the road bends sharp right, take the signed bridleway on the left, leading Northwards. This route appears little used and consequently may be somewhat overgrown. Pass through a small gate and continue alongside the mixed woodland of larch, rowans and oaks. Another gate leads into a field where a blue waymarker indicates straight ahead. The path becomes a wide track and a further gate is reached.

Through the gate descend towards Hanger Farm, bearing NNW, before the buildings, onto a grassy track. Keep this course to follow a path under some trees to a gate where blue waymarking arrows indicate the way ahead.

This hedge path becomes a wide track and expansive views open upon the left. During the Spring and Summer months expect to see a number of different butterflies, including peacock, small heath, speckled wood and gatekeeper, attracted by the wildflowers along this track. Prior to Barleycorn Farm buildings, a wooden gate gives access to a fenced track. Turn right along this track to a gate exiting onto a minor road.

Turn left along the road and after a short distance, turn left onto the metalled lane leading to the Devon and Somerset Gliding Club; this is also signposted as a public bridleway. A long walk along a shaded lane leads to the airfield and club house. Once into the Gliding Club bounds; bear left to pass the club house on the right. Keep to the edge of the field and continue until a path leaves the airfield to the left (SW), immediately prior to a large clump of conifer trees.

Locate two large gateposts bearing blue waymarking arrows and follow the path to the left through these posts. The way continues through a gate and there is woodland both sides of the path. Emerging from the trees to the left there is a marvellous view over fields to Broadhembury, with the church tower providing an excellent landmark.

Shortly cross a track coming in from the right, then take a path indicated over a stile on the left; cross the field to another stile and enter a small clump of trees. Exit into a field and, keeping the hedge left, walk to the corner of this field to climb a stile and follow the signed footpath into another field. Walk straight across this field to a further stile and from this point Broadhembury can be clearly seen.

The village dates from Saxon times, although there was a settlement at Hembury Fort (1 mile South of the village) during the Neolithic period. The surviving earthworks date from the Iron Age. In 1603 the village became part of the Drewe Estate and this association continued for about 300 years. The 'Drewe Arms' reflects this association, although the building predates the 17th century.

Descend the right hand side of this field to the gateway on the far side of the field. This gate exits onto a metalled track at Hembercombe.

Turn right along the track to pass Hembercombe Cottage and a handful of other properties. Shortly a ford is reached on the left; this is a tributary to the River Tale, which name is thought to mean *'quick, active or swift'*, and was mentioned in Domesday.

Cross the bridge to walk back into the village with its attractive thatched cottages.

*see Newton Poppleford walk

★   ★   ★

BRANSCOMBE - STREET

Distance:	Approx. 3½ miles
Time:	Allow 2 - 3 hours
Map:	OS Landranger 192; Pathfinder 08/18
Start reference:	SY195884
Terrain:	Narrow lanes, woodland and cliff paths; one steep climb
Nearest Town:	Sidmouth
Parking:	Village Hall car park, Branscombe
Refreshments:	Beach cafe & Masons Arms, Branscombe
Church:	St. Winifred, Branscombe
Connection:	Sir Nicholas Wadham (died 1610)* Founder of Wadham College, Oxford

Within the tiny church of St. Winifred stands a monument to the mother of Sir Nicholas Wadham, who founded Wadham College in 1616. Edge Barton, to the North of the village of Branscombe, was the Wadham family Dower House and here it was that Joan Wadham came in her Widowhood and later Dame Dorothy Wadham, to whom fell the task of administering the provisions of her husband's will for the establishment of the college, (completed in 1614) for the sum of £14,000.

Turn left on leaving the car park and walk through the village, passing attractive cottages and gardens with lilacs, wiegela and honeysuckle scenting the air in Springtime. When a bend in the road is reached bear right (signposted Beer) and opposite the Mason's Arms turn right along the road indicated to the beach. Pass the old vicarage and pause a while to look back down the valley and pick out the church; across the valley's patchwork of fields is a ridge of woodland through which this walk will pass.

The road narrows as it descends to the beach at Branscombe Mouth so that care should be taken along this stretch. With the car park and cafe on the right, cross the small foot-bridge and follow the road past the cafe. Immediately after the cafe bear right, climb the stile and follow the signposted footpath running diagonally (West) across the field. A gateway into a second field is reached and from this point look up to see a small gate in the hedge on the opposite side of this field - make for this gate.

Passing through the gate steps lead away to the right; before continuing, climb the steps ahead to a vantage point from where you can look to the left to see Hooken Cliffs on the other side of Branscombe Mouth - 200 years ago these cliffs were the scene of a major landslide when 10 acres of land plunged into the sea.

Regain the path and commence the steep climb up West Cliff. The path leads through mixed woodland containing rowan, hawthorn, and elder trees with the floor being a carpet of bluebells and wild garlic, while the path is lined by campion, primroses and dog's mercury in season. The path levels, the walking is easier and a stile is reached leading into a field, giving a view down the combe to Branscombe.

Continue along the stony path, eventually leaving West Cliff behind; climb a stile and enter more woodland where the path becomes level walking and the trees provide welcome shade from the sun on a hot day.

This woodland is home to many birds, including pied wagtails, chaffinches and blackbirds. The call of the pheasant, the laugh of the green woodpecker or even the harsh call of the buzzard may be heard.

A point is reached on the right where the trees thin out a little, enabling a birds-eye view of St. Winifred's church and glimpses of the attractive gardens in the village below. The path continues as a wide track and shortly a signpost is reached indicating "Branscombe (Street) ½ mile". Undertake this walk in May and enjoy the almond scent from the profusion of hawthorn blossom along this part of the route.

St. Winifred's - Branscombe.

Shortly a yellow arrow indicates the way to Street, leading right (West) along a well distinguished grassy track, offering views over Branscombe to the right. The track bears left into a field. Keeping the hedgerow on the right, follow this line to a stile where the way drops down through Pit Coppice, consisting of more mixed woodland - including hazel and beech - and where there is an abundance of yellow rattle, daffodils, bluebells, violets, primroses, spurge, wild chervil, hogweed and wild garlic in Spring and Summer. Here may be found butterflies such as the tortoiseshell, red admiral and gatekeeper from April to September.

The path is stony and descends sharply through the woods to another stile. The descent continues through a field and over a stile onto a narrow path passing between a small garden on the left and a cottage on the right. Pass through a gate onto a metalled road into the hamlet of Street.

Turn right here and walk to a T-junction, turning right again to return to Branscombe. This road takes you past thatched cottages with a wonderful array of tubs, boxes and hanging baskets overflowing with colour in the Summer. As well as the cottages to be admired, there are wonderful open views ahead.

Continue along this road to the church of St. Winifred, which nestles below the road level. There has been a church here since Saxon times, although the main building dates from around the 12th century with additions and alterations being made in the following four centuries. Walking down the path a red horse chestnut tree and two ancient yew trees are passed. On entering the church note the 15th century mural on the wall opposite, uncovered during restoration work in 1911-12, and passing into the transepts and chancel look up to the wagon roof; this dates from the 14th century and consists of about 200 yards of oak beams. As well as the impressive Wadham family memorial there is the 18th century three-decker pulpit, one of only two in Devon.

On the opposite side of the road to the church is a 13th century house called Church Living which was used by the Canons of Exeter Cathedral as a Summer residence, but which is now a private house.

Continue along the road to the thatched forge, with its open fire and hand bellows, and opposite, the bakery where the bread is baked in ovens heated by ash faggots; both these properties are now owned by the National Trust. The village hall and car park are on the left just after the forge.

* see Knowstone walk

★   ★   ★

SALCOMBE REGIS - TROW
VIA DUNSCOMBE

Distance:	Approx. 3½ miles
Time:	Allow 2 - 3 hours
Map:	OS Landranger 192; Pathfinder 08/18
Start reference:	SY147888
Terrain:	Field paths, cliff paths & minor roads
Nearest Town:	Sidmouth
Parking:	Salcombe Regis church
Church:	St. Mary & St. Peter, Salcombe Regis
Connection:	Sir John Ambrose Fleming (1849 - 1945) Inventor of the Radio Valve Sir Joseph Norman Lockyer (1836 -1920) Founder of the Salcombe Hill Observatory

Lying at peace in this churchyard are two brilliant men who between them did much to advance the cause of engineering and science.

Sir John Ambrose Fleming was born at Lancaster and became an engineer and scientist. In 1881 he joined the Edison Electrical Lighting Company, from St. John's College, Cambridge. It was in 1904 that he patented the thermionic electron tube for radio use and in 1910 he became Professor of Electrical Engineering at University College, London. He was a pioneer in the application of electricity to heating and lighting and remained in business as a consultant engineer, devoting much attention to radio-telegraphy.

Sir Norman Lockyer initially pursued astronomy in his leisure time, then in 1870 he was appointed Secretary to the Royal Commission on Scientific Instruction and the Advancement of Science. Between 1870 and 1905 he led eight eclipse expeditions on behalf of the British Government, resigning from the Astro-physics Observatory at South Kensington in 1913 to become the director of the Salcombe Hill Observatory, which is now known as the Norman Lockyer Observatory in his memory. He died at Salcombe Regis on 16th August 1920.

Leave the church and turn left (South) along the road signposted to the beach. This road leads downhill past attractive cottages and gardens, becoming an unmade stony track leading to Coombe Wood House and Farm. The track is lined by sycamore, chestnut and elder trees with the banks full of nettles, bluebells and campion, attracting many butterflies, such as the orange-tip and peacock during the Spring and Summer. Buzzards, woodpeckers and pheasants may be heard calling.

The track leads between two houses and through a gate where the path divides. Take the path signposted to the left (SSE) and climb steeply. Pause on the way up to admire the view and on reaching the summit it is possible on a clear day to see the coastlines of Sidmouth, Budleigh Salterton and Exmouth.

Bear left (NE) and continue climbing between hawthorn trees, massed with almond-scented blossom in May. In Spring and Summer there are more bluebells and primroses here as well as stitchwort, lesser celandines and creeping or common bugle. When the track levels look for a large oak tree on the right with a stile beneath.

Climb the stile into a field and keeping a NE course pass through the gate at the far end of the field and continue straight on through the next field. A gate is reached by farm buildings, where the path turns left. Walk to the corner of the field and turn right. At the end of this path there is a stile leading onto a wide track, offering a choice of three routes.

Turn immediately right (SSE) on leaving the field and follow the grassy track between high hedges. After a short distance a stile is reached on the left leading into National Trust land entitled Lincombe. The way ahead is a level grassy path through an avenue of rowan trees. Walking on, a signpost is reached indicating Weston Mouth straight ahead and from this point onwards the

St. Mary & St. Peter - Salcombe Regis.

views from this cliff-top path become quite breathtaking.

This is a wonderful place to sit for a while and breathe in the sea air and admire the undulating coastline. The air, in May, is scented with the blossom of the many hawthorn trees along this path; this lightly wooded area attracts many birds, as well as butterflies and day flying moths, such as the speckled yellow - a most striking and beautiful moth. Later in the year, pyramid orchids can be found along the cliff-top.

After a short distance a stile is reached and the path continues along the cliff-top, descending gradually and then bearing left into woodland. Yellow arrows indicate the route to take. Two steps take the path to a junction, turn left here and when the path joins a wider track turn right.

This track leads through Dunscombe Manor Caravan Park and Dunscombe Coppice. The woodland floor is carpeted by blue-bells and wild garlic in season with numerous wild flowers, such as campion stitchwort, dog's mercury, yellow rattle, spurge, speedwell and wild strawberries.

Continue climbing through the Park to a metal gate onto a road. Turn right here and walk up the road between high hedgerows and banks made colourful with numerous wild flowers - the sound of donkeys' braying may be heard. Gateways are passed on the right through which the source of the commotion may be seen. After a short distance a signposted footpath (to Weston Mouth) and a stile are reached on the right and this path leads into the Donkey Sanctuary.

Take time to visit the Sanctuary - over 5000 donkeys have now been helped by this Sanctuary and valuable aid is being given to Third World Countries where the donkey is often the only source of transport. The Sanctuary is open from 9 am to dusk every day of the year, and a very comprehensive information centre can be visited.

Leaving the Sanctuary by the main entrance, turn left and then right (West) onto a signposted footpath to Trow. Walk along the side of the field keeping the hedge on the right. A gate is reached into a second field, walk straight across the field to a gate in the opposite hedgerow. There are open views all around to the distant hills; when the gate is reached, turn right along the footpath to Trow. Walk straight on through the next field to a gate alongside a thatched farmhouse, exiting onto a track. The way ahead is past cottages with attractive gardens.

Follow the track to its junction with a metalled road and turn left. After a short distance, pass the Salcombe Regis Caravan and Camping site.

Descending the hill a large hawthorn tree is seen. This is the Salcombe Regis Thorn and the legend on a stone tablet informs us that '*A hawthorn tree has been maintained here since Saxon times when it marked the boundary between the cultivated field of the combe and the open common of the hill. It has given the name Thorn to the adjacent house, where a Manor Court was held, and to the surrounding farm*'.

At Thorn Cross junction turn left to descend Soldiers Hill and the church will shortly be seen. Pass through the lych-gate to visit this tiny church where the visitor is always welcome. The graves of Sir John Ambrose Fleming and Sir Norman Lockyer are to the South side of the church. Inside the church there are numerous memorial plaques on the walls of the chancel and in the South aisle, as well as two memorial windows. The church dates from the 12th century but additions and alterations were made during the following three centuries. It is hard to imagine the War coming to this peaceful place but in 1942 a bomb blew out the South window, which was then replaced by clearer glass. Notice the tapestried kneelers depicting scenes of village life as well as the Thorn tree at the top of Soldiers Hill.

★   ★   ★

NEWTON POPPLEFORD - HARPFORD & BEACON HILL

Distance:	Approx. 5½ miles
Time:	Allow 4 hours
Map:	OS Landranger 192 Pathfinder SY 09/19 & SY 08/18
Start reference:	SY086897
Terrain:	Stony tracks, field and woodland paths; one steep climb.
Nearest Town:	Sidmouth
Parking:	Free car park, Newton Poppleford
Refreshments:	Several places in Newton Poppleford, Bowd Inn
Church:	St. Gregory's, Harpford
Connection:	Rev. Augustus Montague Toplady (1740-1778)* Writer of hymn *'Rock of Ages'*

The Reverend Toplady was Vicar at St. Gregory's from 1766 - 1768. There is a cross in the churchyard which stands as a memorial to him, being restored in his memory in 1913. An inscription around the base is a quote from his hymn *'Rock of Ages'*. The cross is sited on the remains of a much older cross and it may be said of it that is is a *'Rock of Ages'*. In 1768 he took the living of Broadhembury

From the car park walk down to the main road, turn right and cross the road to walk along to Back Lane. Into Back Lane and continue past the recreation ground until a signposted footpath on the right is reached. The path is on the course of the now dismantled railway line and follows alongside the River Otter. Look out for indian balsam growing along the banks of the river in Summer.

Cross the River via the footbridge, climb two stiles and a track leads to the minor road through the village of Harpford. Turn left

St. Gregories - Harpford.

along the road to a T-junction beside the church. Left again, then right up Knapps Lane. This is a metalled lane, narrow, with high banks playing host to many different kinds of ferns.

Pass the signposted footpath to Bowd and continue uphill; the lane gives way to a stony track and the route to Harpford Wood is indicated (½ mile). Cross the dismantled railway line via an old brick-built bridge and the path then narrows considerably. There are high hedgerows each side, providing welcome shade on a sunny day.

A stile is reached from where there is a good view across to Harpford Wood. The path continues until a kissing gate is reached, once through the gate the path swings right (East). Before proceeding, stop for a moment to take in the view across the valley ahead towards Tipton St. John. The path winds its way upwards, again under trees, emerging into a field. Keep ENE along the top edge of the field, heading towards woodland. At the far end of the field another kissing gate leads into Harpford Wood, with its noble oaks and ancient beeches.

Into the wood, turn left (East) along a wide track. The sound of donkeys' braying may be heard. This comes from Woods Farm, which is shortly passed on the left. Woods Farm is owned by the Donkey Sanctuary, Sidmouth, and is home to over 300 donkeys. It was in 1987 that the Sanctuary rescued Blackie from Villaneuva De La Vera, Spain, following the village's annual fiesta. He now lives happily at the Sanctuary, but the struggle to stop the donkey's suffering during this fiesta continues.

Do not take the footpath leading up to the car park, but continue for a short distance, passing a second exit, to a path which exits onto the B3176. Take great care in crossing the road to join the path indicated to 'Fire Beacon', which is directly opposite. Take a NE course to climb the side of this field, continuing upwards to a second field. This is a steep climb but immensely rewarding with its views to Sidmouth and the sea beyond, Newton Poppleford and the surrounding countryside. At the top of this field bear right and follow the hedge along for a short distance until steps in the hedge-bank are reached; a stile leads onto a minor road.

Turn left along this narrow road and walk with care in case of traffic. Pass a gate on the left, from where you have a grandstand view over Woods Farm and the donkeys. Just after this gate, a signposted footpath on the right leads through woodland along the foot of Beacon Hill, heading NNE. This is a pleasant path beneath deciduous trees, which include sycamore, oak and beech. Foxgloves and honeysuckle make this a most attractive walk in Summer.

The path exits briefly into a narrow field, before passing a house to the left and climbing once again beside the woodland. A point is reached where several paths converge; turn right to join a wide track and then right (SSE) again. This wide stony track eventually leads back into woodland. When the track divides, keep to the left-hand fork. Once again the surroundings are extremely pleasant; this is light open woodland providing a home for many ferns on the woodland floor.

Some distance along this track a junction of paths is reached, take the path on the right through an avenue of trees. On emerging from the trees there is a magnificent view to Sidmouth. Continue along this path to a junction with a bridleway. Turn left and descend the bridleway through the heather, gorse and bracken. At the next junction, turn left again and continue the descent; pass a turning on the right and the way becomes less distinguished. The path enters woodland and here be prepared for some boggy areas; this part of the route provides a wealth of fungi in Autumn. Fallen trees may be across the path in places, but the route follows a generally SSE course. There are glimpses of the sea, Bulverton Hill and Peak Hill away to the right.

Just before the edge of this woodland is reached look for a path on the right leading WSW downhill between fields. Again the path may be partially obscured by undergrowth. A point is reached where the path divides. Take the right hand path indicated across a field and exit into a farm yard. Follow the track through the yard and onto a metalled lane. Continue on to a minor road and bear left along the road (Fire Beacon Lane).

This road ends at a T-junction with the B3176. Here turn left and cross the road to locate the footpath to Harpford on the right, just before the Bowd Inn. The return route to Harpford lies along the course of the dismantled railway. An embankment is passed which supports many kinds of ferns, and the path is lined by deciduous trees.

Emerging from this woodland continue along the track until a fork on the right is reached. Take this path which leads back to the railway bridge crossed on the outward route. Retrace the outward route to the commencement of Knapps Lane. Turn left and walk down the road to enter the churchyard by the side gate; ahead now is the monument to the Reverend Toplady. Enter this much restored church and notice the beautiful stained glass windows. The oldest part of the church is the base of the font believed to be Norman, with the tower dating from the 15th century.

Leave the church by the main entrance, passing the paved area to the right where the Church House once stood. Walk back through the village and re-cross the River Otter, retracing the outward route along Back Lane to return to the car park.

* see Broadhembury walk

★   ★   ★

All Saints - East Budleigh.

EAST BUDLEIGH - YETTINGTON

VIA HAYES BARTON

Distance:	3½ miles
Time:	Allow 2 - 3 hours
Map:	OS Landranger 192; Pathfinder SY08/18
Start reference:	SY066849
Terrain:	Lanes and field paths
Nearest Town:	Budleigh Salterton
Parking:	Free car park in Hayes Lane, East Budleigh
Refreshments:	East Budleigh
Church:	All Saints, East Budleigh
Connection:	Sir Walter Raleigh (1552 - 1618)
	Soldier, sailor, politician & author

East Budleigh is the birth-place of Sir Walter Raleigh and this walk encompasses the old vicarage where Raleigh was educated, the Tudor farmhouse where he was born and the magnificent church where he worshipped. Raleigh, who introduced potatoes and tobacco into Britain, was knighted in 1584 and appointed Vice-Admiral of Devon and Cornwall in 1585. He wrote a number of historical works as well as poems, the most notable of these being *'The Pilgrimage'* and *'The Lie'*.

From the car park turn right (West) and continue along Hayes Lane, where the hedges in the Spring and Summer months are rich with wild flowers, including green alkanet, yarrow, vetch, speedwell, foxgloves and honeysuckle. Cross the Budleigh Brook, a tributary to the River Otter, and soon is passed Vicar's Mead (left), where the young Walter Raleigh was tutored by the Reverend John Ford. Look for a turning on the left (South) in the form of a rough track which climbs steeply at its commencement.

When the track begins to descend locate the signposted foot-path to the right (West) climbing alongside a field hedge made colourful by poppies, toadflax, wall pennywort, and field scabious in season. The path climbs quite steeply and views of the surrounding countryside open up; look back to see the church tower at East Budleigh. Follow the path, keeping the hedge on the left until a stile is reached into a second field.

Once over the stile, turn left (SW) and again follow the hedge line down the field passing a small brick-built enclosed reservoir. At the bottom of the field turn right and walk along the hedge line, through fields, until another metal gate is reached with a footpath sign alongside. Exit into the narrow grassy lane and turn right (West).

After a short distance a point is reached where a narrow path, leading NW, enters woodland on the right. Once into the woodland rejoin a wide track and follow a NW course to a point where the path turns right (North). At this point the route is way marked. The path descends rapidly and here the banks are clothed by fine mosses and delicate ferns.

Leave the woods, passing a house on the left, and continue along the track leading away from the house to is junction with a minor road. At the minor road a footpath is indicated into the opposite field, but before continuing on this route, turn left and walk along the road for a short distance to Hayes Barton - Walter Raleigh's birth-place. This privately owned farmhouse, with gables and mullioned windows, is well preserved.

Retrace footsteps to the stile and follow the path along the edge of the field, keeping the hedge on the right. Pass through two more fields and a stile is reached leading onto a minor road. Turn right (NE) along this road edged by sweet chestnut and birch trees. When a T-junction is reached, again turn right (ESE) and follow the road through the small village of Yettington with its attractive thatched dwellings and cottage gardens. This is a minor, but well used, road.

Shortly after leaving the village, the entrance to Bicton Park is passed (left). Progress along the road gives sight of East Budleigh

Hayes Barton - birthplace of Sir Walter Raleigh.

church tower. The road descends gradually as it re-enters East Budleigh and as it does so, a wrought iron gate is reached leading into the churchyard of All Saints.

This interesting church contains memorials to the Raleigh family and there is a portrait of Sir Walter Raleigh hanging in the North aisle, close to the Raleigh family pew. Set into the floor of the nave, in front of the chancel screen, is a slab of dark grey stone bearing a cross - this is the tomb of Joan Raleigh, first wife of Walter Raleigh (Sir Walter's father). Of considerable note are the carved bench ends - the Raleigh family pew is decorated with the family coat of arms - and the colourful roof bosses. The kneelers are indeed works of art, depicting features both inside the church and around the village.

The churchyard offers a view Southwards towards Vicar's Mead and Hayes Wood, which has doubtless changed little since the days when the young Walter Raleigh trod this hallowed ground.

From the main gateway to the church, the car park is but a few yards distant.

★   ★   ★

WOLBOROUGH - ABBOTSKERSWELL - DECOY

Distance:	Approx. 4 miles
Time:	Allow 2 - 3 hours
Map:	OS Landranger 202; Pathfinder SX87/97 & SX 86/96
Start reference:	SX854704
Terrain:	Field and woodland paths, some minor roads; gentle climbs
Nearest Town:	Newton Abbot
Parking:	Church at Wolborough
Church:	St. Mary's, Wolborough
Connection:	John Lethbridge (Died 1759) Inventor of a diving engine

Although there is no longer a marked grave in the churchyard, it is recorded in the church register that John Lethbridge, who lived in Newton Abbot and was a feofee of the church (a holder of land granted by the church), was buried on the 11th December 1759. It was in 1715 that he produced his diving apparatus, which consisted of a leather barrel with two sleeves for the arms and an observation porthole. It is said that he made a considerable fortune from his invention by recovering from the seabed, in different parts of the world, almost £100,000 for the Dutch and English merchants which had been lost by shipwreck.

From the church, cross the road to the signposted footpath leading South into a field. Walk straight ahead to a gap in the hedge and take a SSE course across the next field, to the far right hand corner where there is a stile.

Pause before leaving this field to admire the view across Newton Abbot. It's possible to see the church at Highweek, away to the North, with the large communities of Kingsteignton and Bishopsteignton to the North-East.

Exit onto the road and turn left following the road for about a mile. Care must be taken along this narrow but busy road. When a property called Crystalwood is reached, the footpath into the village of Abbotskerswell is just a few yards along on the right.

Bear left (South) over the stile, keeping to the top of the field and walk towards the houses. Shortly a stile is reached leading into a cul-de-sac serving these houses. Continue down to the road and turn left along Manor Road. When a junction is reached bear left up Priory Road. A steady climb but one with lovely views over the village of Abbotskerswell.

Part way along this road there is a commemorative seat to George V, which states '1910 - 1935 God Save The King'. Take a rest on this seat and admire the view.

Further long the road narrows and then appears to widen, with a lay-by on the left. Locate the public footpath on the left over a stile into a field. Take a NE course across the field towards a broken down farm building to locate a stile into the next field. Continue on the same course across this next field to a stile in the hedgerow, and cross the small footbridge over the stream running between the fields. Cross the corner of this field to a stile set up in the hedgerow to the right. Over this stile follow the line of the hedge to a stile exiting onto a wide track at the corner of Blackball Plantation.

Take the wide track straight ahead alongside the plantation. In Autumn the track is carpeted in leaves, the golden brown of oak, the shiny coppery coloured beech and the yellowing hazel. A few fungi may also be found. Keep along this track until a stile is reached on the left and the footpath enters Blackball Plantation.

When a division is reached in the path, take the right hand path down steps, passing a large pond. The path exits into a large recreation field. Keeping the hedge and fence on the left walk around the edge of this field. Pass a picnic area and shortly the car park and play area at Decoy is seen.

St. Mary's - Wolborough

Continue on the wide path passing Decoy Lake on the left. Here expect to see swans, geese and ducks. Follow the path past the sailing club and enter woodland again. After a small stone bridge is crossed the path shortly joins a wide track. Turn right along the track to a kissing-gate and a footpath sign.

Bear left to enter a field and the way runs beside a small stream. Here there are goat willows and silver birch, and a magnificent oak. The path leads to another kissing-gate and exits beside a wide track. Turn right along the track and continue up to the road.

Turn left along the road, taking care along this well-used route. Enter the churchyard at the first gate and walk up through to the West door of the church. If the church is locked, obtain the key from the farm opposite.

This is a large, beautifully maintained church. The brass plaques and copper jug are evidence of much dedicated polishing. The painted and gilded screens and the stained glass windows do much to make this church bright and welcoming. In the chancel there is a dominating marble memorial to Sir Richard and Lady Lucy Reynell. Sir Richard Reynell was a lawyer and two large standing figures appear on the memorial: Justice and Time. Sir Richard Reynell built Forde House (1610) in Newton Abbot (now home to Teignbridge District Council) whilst Lady Reynell founded a hospital in this parish in 1638 for poor clergymen's widows.

★   ★   ★

WIDECOMBE - GRIMSPOUND - THORNEYHILL LANE - BONEHILL

Distance:	Approx. 7½ miles
Time:	Allow 5 hours
Map:	OS Landranger 202; Outdoor Leisure 28; Pathfinder SX67/77 & SX68/78
Start reference:	SX719768
Terrain:	Rough tracks, moorland & roads. Not to be undertaken in poor visibility.
Nearest Town:	Ashburton
Parking:	Car park, Widecombe
Refreshments:	Rugglestone Inn & Old Inn, Widecombe
Church:	St. Pancras, Widecombe-in-the-Moor
Connection:	Olive Katherine Parr (1874 - 1955) Author of Beatrice Chase

Buried in the churchyard is Olive Katherine Parr, who lived at nearby Venton House for over 50 years, where she had her own Catholic Chapel. A prolific writer, her works included *'Devon and Heaven'* and *'Through a Dartmoor Window'*, which contained a strong religious element, and she was the founder of the *'Crusade for White Knights and Ladies'*. She felt strongly about the preservation of Dartmoor, and became Vice-President of the SW Division of the League against Cruel Sports.

❖   ❖   ❖

Turn right out of the car park and walk straight to the junction with the minor road to Natsworthy. Turn right along this road and after a small footbridge (right), turn left up Church Lane, a steep metalled track signposted Hameldown for Grimspound. This track becomes stony and wet as it approaches the edge of the moor.

St. Pancras - Widecombe-in-the-Moor.

At the top of Church Lane, bear right (NNW) up the side of the moor, keeping the stone wall to the right. After passing a sign denoting *'Path to Widecombe'* the track forks, here bear slightly right again (NW) onto the Two Moors Way, leading to the top of Hameldown and its Beacon. As a guide to reaching Hameldown Beacon, look for the enclosure wall from Blackaton Manor Farm (left), which climbs the hillside and ends at the Beacon. The stone indicating the Beacon announces it as Hamilton Beacon. Pause for a moment here to take in the view.

From Hameldown Beacon, the next landmarks are Two Barrows, Single Barrow and Broad Barrow. Two Barrows and Single Barrow are to the left of the path, both indicated by a stone marker similar to that on Hameldown Beacon.

In the years 1872 and 1873, these Barrows were excavated and revealed small amounts of burnt human bones. The most exciting find was the bronze blade of a dagger together with the amber pommel inlaid with gold. From this lofty elevation there are few prominent heights within the Dartmoor region that cannot be seen. It is possible to see Dartmoor's three forestry plantations from here - Bellever, Soussons and Fernworthy (left to right).

Broad Barrow is seen ahead on the horizon. Pass to the left of Broad Barrow (NW) and the remains of Hameldown Cross are reached after about mile. This is just another boundary stone on which will be found the date 1854 and the letters D.S., standing for Duke of Somerset, a former owner of Natsworthy Manor.

From the Cross it is possible to see the next landmark which is the triangulation cone on the top of Hameldown Tor (Hameldown Tor is the highest point on Hameldown). Continue straight on to a boulder strewn path which takes you down to Grimspound, set out below in all its glory. This enclosure covers an area of approximately 4 acres, has a circumference of 500 yards and contains ruins of 24 hut circles.

Grimspound was the venue chosen by the Mothers from Widecombe for their summer picnic in Eden Philpott's *'Widecombe Fair'*, and where they were later to receive a lecture on this primaeval village from a most learned resident - so solemn was this discourse that many of them succumbed to the heat of the day and fell asleep.

Leave Grimspound along the Easterly path and follow the wide track which climbs steadily. A conifer plantation will shortly be seen on the left. Follow the line of the trees down (ESE) to arrive at Natsworthy Gate.

Pause as you walk along this wide track and take in the panorama - Moretonhampstead can be seen with Easdon Tor to the right; to the left, further distant, is Castle Drogo. Later Honeybag and Chinkwell Tors, Hound Tor, Haytor and Rippon Tor can all be seen.

Pass through the gate and turn right down the road towards Widecombe. After about mile a cattle grid is reached, shortly after Isaford Farm. Immediately after this grid, turn left (ESE) and climb the rough steep track leading up from the road. On reaching the gate turn right onto Thorneyhill Lane, which runs beside a conifer plantation and below Honeybag and Chinkwell Tors. This lane exits onto a road just below Bonehill Rocks.

At the road turn right between stone gateposts and follow the road down to a small bridge over the East Webburn River. At the T-junction turn right and return to Widecombe.

Possibly the best known feature of Widecombe is its large perpendicular style church, which has become known as the *'Cathedral of the Moor'*. It was built by tin miners to give thanks for their prosperity. Its tower is recognisable from miles around, standing 120 feet high, topped by four pinnacles supporting four crosses. Inside only the base of the 15th century screen has survived, depicting some 32 saints, of which St. Pancras is one. The church suffered considerable damage in October 1638 when it was struck by lightning during a violent thunderstorm. It is recorded that 4 persons were killed and 62 injured.

NEW BRIDGE - HOLNE MOOR
VIA HOLNE & MICHELCOMBE

Distance:	Approx. 7½ miles
Time:	Allow 5 hours
Map:	OS Landranger 202; Outdoor Leisure 28; Pathfinder SX66/76 & SX67/77
Start reference:	SX713708
Terrain:	Well used paths, road and moorland; steep climbs & streams to ford.
Nearest Town:	Ashburton
Parking:	Car park at New Bridge
Refreshments:	Church House Inn, Holne; Old Forge Tea-Rooms, Holne
Church:	St. Mary the Virgin, Holne
Connection:	Charles Kingsley (1819 -1875) Author 'The Water Babies', 'Westward Ho!' & 'Hereward the Wake'.

Charles Kingsley was born in Holne, his father then being the Curate in Charge. Following his education at Kings College, Cambridge, he followed in his father's footsteps and was ordained. He was first Curate and then Rector at Eversley in Hampshire. It was during his lifelong pastorate here that he wrote *Westward Ho!*, which reflected his thoughts on his Devonshire boyhood. His time spent at Holne was not forgotten, and a memorial window was placed in the church in 1894.

From the car park cross New Bridge and turn right through a lay-by to a stile onto a path through Cleave Wood. In Springtime the primroses, violets and bluebells make quite a show here. Keep alongside the River Dart as it gurgles and splashes over the boulders in its path. When the path divides, bear left away from the River.

Climb through the woodland to a gate into a field, keeping along the top of the field to a stile on the left. Over this stile, climb steeply to a further stile in the field corner which exits into a hedged path. Follow this path to another stile and a minor road.

Church House Inn - Holne

Turn left along the road, then right to descend to Holne Village. At the next road junction, cross straight over passing the Church House Inn, Church and Tea-Rooms on the right. The Inn dates from 1329 and Cromwell is said to have stayed here. The screen in the lounge bar came from the church and is 300 - 400 years old.

This road passes attractive cottages and gardens to arrive at Play Cross. Turn left along the road to Scorriton and after Littlecombe Farm bear right along the road to Michelcombe. Through this hamlet, pass a bridge on the right and follow the road ahead signposted *'Bridlepath only'*.

Arriving at a metal gate pass through and turn right along the path indicated to Holne Moor via Great Combe. Shortly after Great Combe the path swings right and there is a stream to be forded. Continue up the valley keeping the stream on the left.

Pass through a wooden gate, climb steeply and shortly pass *'Glen Rowan'*. The path swings sharp left (signposted) and continues climbing to a small gate by a summer house, arriving at open moorland. Follow the gulley straight ahead and when it disappears continue in a Northerly direction, to arrive at Holne Town Leat flowing E-W (supplies water to Holne village, farms and surrounding fields). Find a convenient point to cross and continue in the same direction. A bridge will shortly become visible to the right and a wide grassy track is reached. Here turn left and cross the Holne Moor Leat, flowing North to South, which carries water from the Wo Brook to the Holy Brook and supplies water to Buckfastleigh.

From this point there are magnificent views to Princetown and the masts atop North Hessary Tor are visible on the skyline.

The track crosses the Holne Moor Leat twice more by means of small bridges and continues with a stone wall to the left. At the end of this wall there are the spoil heaps of the long-deserted Ringleshutts open-cast tin mine.

There was a house at Ringleshutts connected with the mine and its occupation continued after the mine closed, but it was burned down many years ago; the children of the house accidentally set fire to it whilst their parents were absent.

Bear to the left of these workings and a short distance ahead is seen the dry channel of Wheal Emma Leat. Keeping this to the left take a SW course to the top of the ridge ahead. Cross the ridge and turn left onto a wide grassy track running downhill. This is Sandy Way. From here there are views over Michelcombe, Scorriton and Holne.

Follow this track down to the gate at Lane Head. This stony track leads back to the metal gate at Michelcombe where the outward route is retraced as far as the stone bridge; here turn left into Michelcombe Lane. A steady climb ends at a T-junction. Cross the road and pass through a metal kissing-gate, where there is a house to the right. Walk straight across the field to a second kissing-gate leading into the churchyard.

The church dates from the 13th century, with additions in the 15th century. The North window is of stained glass and a memorial to Charles Kingsley, baptised in this church when his father was Curate in Charge. The screen depicts forty figures along the base and the top is ornately carved with wheat and grapes, with birds stealing the grapes. In the churchyard, by the door, stands the dole stone, which was formerly used for dispensing charity.

Leaving the church via the main gate, turn left along the road, once again passing the Church House Inn. Straight across at the

Hannaford Manor.

junction, continuing along the road to a T-junction. Turn right (NNE) to ascend the hill. Take a rest on the Coronation Seat and admire the marvellous view across Dartmoor from here. At the top of the hill take the road signed to Hembury on the right.

A fairly level walk leads to Gallant Le Bower Cross. Here take the left fork and descend to a junction, bearing right along the road. Extreme care must be taken on this narrow section of road. Pass Chase Gate Farm and take the signposted footpath leading westwards. From this stile it is possible to look across to Hannaford Manor, among the trees, which was designed by Sir Edward Lutyens and built between 1904 and 1911.

The path runs along the right hand side of the field and passes through a hedge into a second field. Descend along the right hand side of this field to a stile in the corner and exit onto the road. Turn left along the road to New Bridge and the car park.

HOLNE - LITTLECOMBE - LANGAFORD

VIA CHALK FORD

Distance:	Approx. 5 miles
Time:	Allow 3½ hours
Map:	OS Landranger 202; Outdoor Leisure 28; Pathfinder SX66/76
Start reference:	SX705696
Terrain:	Minor roads, stony tracks, fields and moorland
Nearest Town:	Ashburton
Parking:	Holne car park
Refreshments:	Church House Inn, Holne. Tradesman's Arms, Scorriton
Church:	St. Mary the Virgin, Holne
Connection:	Charles Kingsley (1819 -1875) Author 'The Water Babies', 'Westward Ho!' and 'Hereward the Wake'.

Note: As Holne and the surrounding countryside is such an attractive area for walking, it was impossible not to include this second walk based on the church at Holne. For information about Charles Kingsley and details of the church, please refer to walk 8.

From the car park turn left along the road to arrive at Play Cross; bear left to Scorriton and descend. The road forks right to Michel-combe, but keep left (SW) to descend to Holy Brook Bridge and Scorriton is soon reached.

The first building passed is the Methodist chapel, with its series of foundation stones bearing the names of local benefactors. Continue through this hamlet, passing the Tradesman's Arms, Scorriton Farm and Rosemary Lane. At the top of the hill turn right for Lower and Higher Coombe to descend to Coombe Bridge over the

St. Mary the Virgin - Holne

River Mardle.

Follow the road as it bears to the right and climb slightly. Where the road divides, take the right (West) fork to Higher Coombe. Lakemoor and Scae Wood are seen to the left. With the River Mardle to the right, walk along the road past a number of properties and Mardlewood House is straight ahead. Keep to the left of Great Oak to take the signed track to Lud Gate, which leads through Lakemoor and Scae Wood.

This rough stony track climbs steeply beneath trees offering welcome shade on a hot day. The banks are mossy and covered by ferns, including the hard fern, male fern and lady fern, as well as primroses and toadflax in season. The track enters a field then passes through an avenue of oaks, before continuing uphill between fields. There are good views across the Holy Brook Valley from this track.

The track becomes a path as it enters a field via a stile. Keep to the right-hand side of the field, keeping Scae Wood to the right. At the corner of the field swing SW to climb a second stile into another field. With the hedge to the right continue to a hunting gate on the right.

Pass through this gate, bearing left to exit onto an unmade track via a pair of gates. Turn right along the track to Lud Gate, on the edge of Buckfastleigh moor. There is a signpost here indicating Scorriton to the right. Bear NNE and follow the line of the wall as it descends. Expect to find sheep and ponies grazing amongst the gorse and bracken of the moor.

The wall eventually bears away to the right but continue in the same direction and the path is subsequently joined by a track running in from Warmmacombe. As the path descends to Chalk Ford, once again there are splendid views.

Chalk Ford is the perfect spot to pause a while to watch the wagtails searching for insects and enjoying the water of the River Mardle.

The river is crossed by means of a wooden footbridge. Once over the bridge bear right along the stony track from where there are expansive views. Follow this wide track to the minor road. Turning right and then almost immediately left along a lane, passing the telephone kiosk. At the end of the lane turn left and once more cross the Holy Brook.

Ignore the bridlepath sign on the left, continuing to a rough stony track indicated *'Unsuitable for Motors'*. This is known as Langaford Steep and is the most direct route to Holne. There are high hedges lining the track, but look back occasionally for a wonderful view.

Emerging onto the minor road, just prior to Play Cross, continue straight ahead to return to Play Cross and from there descend to Holne Village. To visit the church continue past the car park to enter via the main gate.

ERMINGTON - KEATON

Distance:	Approx. 4 miles
Time:	Allow 2 - 3 hours
Map:	OS Landranger 202; Pathfinder SX 65/75
Start reference:	SX638532
Terrain:	Country lanes, two field paths; one steep climb
Nearest Town:	Ivybridge
Parking:	Ermington village centre or near church
Refreshments:	Crooked Spire Inn; First & Last Inn, Ermington
Church:	St. Peter and St. Paul, Ermington
Connection:	Miss Violet Alice Pinwill (1874 - 1959) West Country wood-carver

Miss Pinwill was one of seven daughters of the Reverend Edmund Pinwill, who was vicar at Ermington from 1880 - 1924. The church was in a poor state of repair when the Reverend Pinwill arrived and funds were raised for restoration to be carried out.

It was at this time that Mrs Pinwill suggested three of her daughters should receive training in wood-carving and so it was that Violet Pinwill's career began. The massive reredos was carved by Violet Pinwill and she designed the alabaster relief beneath it. The sisters were eventually to form their own Company and employ 29 men; much of the carving in this church is the work of Miss Pinwill and her Company.

Miss Pinwill became a teacher and taught at Plymouth Technical College for many years. She died in Plymouth but is buried in Ermington churchyard.

❖   ❖   ❖

St. Peter & St. Paul - Ermington. Note the crooked spire.

Locate the turning between the church and the village centre and descend the hill to join the B3210. Turn left (East) along the road to cross the bridge over the River Erme. Immediately turn left again along the road to Penquit and Strode House. This land is bordered by the River Erme to the left and the Lud Brook to the right. Butterbur (an old medicinal plant) and harts tongue ferns flourish in the dampness along the banks. The hedgerows along this land are host to common polypody ferns, wall pennywort, violets and primroses.

The road climbs after Strode Lodge and House and a road junction is passed on the right. Continue straight on for a few yards to see two public footpath signs on the left. Take the second of these footpaths. Once into the field bear right to follow the line of the hedge. There are splendid views across to Ugborough Moor from this field.

A gate is reached on the right bearing a yellow waymarking arrow. Go through this gate and walk straight (NNE) across this next field to a gate, exiting onto a minor road. Opposite this gateway stands Penquit Manor. Penquit is a Celtic name, meaning *'end of the wood'*, while many of the surrounding place names in this area are Anglo-Saxon.

Turn left (NNW) down the road to descend past attractive gardens and properties. Keep on this narrow road for a distance of about a mile. After a sharp right hand bend pass the property of Caton to arrive at a T-junction. Turn left along this well-used road to once more cross the River Erme.

Over the bridge bear right along the lane signed to Higher Keaton and continue to a junction on the right; turn here and commence a climb which becomes steeper as the lane progresses. The banks lining this lane contain wild carrot and primroses, as well as harts tongue and male ferns. This lengthy climb rewards with splendid views from the summit.

It's possible to overlook the community of Bittaford and the town of Ivybridge, where can be seen the railway viaduct across the valley and just in front the Stowford Paper Mills (built 1862). Beyond this habitation look up to Harford and Ugborough Moors.

It is above Harford Moor, amongst old tin workings that the River Erme rises and flows through Ivybridge and Ermington on its way to the sea.

This lane ends at a T-junction with a minor road. Turn left along the road to pass the radio/television mast and descend the hill to the village of Ermington. Straight ahead is seen the considerable expanse of Ermington Wood. The road enters the village by the Crooked Spire Inn. Bear left through the village, passing the school, to reach the church.

The church has few of its Norman origins remaining. Its famous feature, the crooked spire, is Early English whilst the remainder of the building is mainly Perpendicular. On entering the church porch look up to the sundial dating from 1766, bearing the words *'with speedy foot the age goes by'*. Inside the porch notice the door which at one time led up stairs to a parvise chamber, where the priest would have lived.

The beautiful carving within the church is undoubtedly its most attractive feature, whilst the canopied tomb in the South chapel, dating from around 1580, is most striking with its brightly painted heraldic shields. There are a number of ledger stones set into the floor of the church, although sadly some are now illegible.

★   ★   ★

BURRATOR - SHEEPSTOR

VIA MEAVY

Distance:	Approx. 5 miles
Time:	Allow 4 hours
Map:	OS Landranger 201 & 202; Outdoor Leisure 28 Pathfinder SX 47/57
Start reference:	SX551680
Terrain:	Woodland & field paths, lanes; one steep climb
Nearest Town:	Tavistock
Parking:	West side of dam, Burrator Reservoir
Refreshments:	Royal Oak, Meavy
Church:	St. Leonard's, Sheepstor
Connection:	Sir James Brooke (1803 -1868) & Sir CharlesBrooke (1829 - 1917), 1st and 2nd White Rajahs of Sarawak

Sir James Brooke became the 1st White Rajah of Sarawak in 1841, being invited to remain in that country, following his help in suppressing the civil war then being fought. He created a model state, though received no assistance from the British Government, despite his requesting it. In 1852 his nephew Charles settled in Sarawak and continued Sir James' work becoming Rajah on the death of his uncle. In 1859 Sir James Brooke purchased Burrator, where he retired in 1863 and died in 1868. These two great men are at rest in the churchyard, Sir James Brooke lies under a large slab of red Aberdeen granite, while his nephew rests under a boulder of Dartmoor granite. Their tombs are enclosed by railings with the coat of arms on the gate.

❖   ❖   ❖

St. Peter - Meavy.

From the dam, take the road (South) to Dousland, turning left along a stony track signposted to Meavy. The track leads into mixed woodland of hazel, birch and oak. When the track bends keep straight on through the woodland, following alongside the dry channel of Plymouth Leat. This 16th century construction supplied Plymouth with its water before the Burrator reservoir was built. It was originally 6 feet wide and 2 feet deep, carrying water 17 miles to Plymouth from the River Meavy.

Keep left (SW) where the path divides and descends. Pass through two gates, continuing on the track through this peaceful woodland. Emerging into a field, cross to the gate leading onto the road. Take the road to Yelverton to arrive in the village of Meavy. On entering the village note the ancient oak which stands outside the church; it is thought to be about 900 years old and some 25 feet in circumference. The 15th century church of St. Peter is well worth a visit. A pier of rose coloured stone in the chancel is carved with heads and an episcopal staff and is part of the earlier Norman building. A slate tombstone in the churchyard, near the chancel wall, commemorates Tregillgus, the village blacksmith, in a rhyming epitaph.

Leave the church and continue along the road to a junction on the left indicated to Hoo Meavy. Cross the bridge and take the signposted path to Lovaton (½ m) along a walled track to emerge into a field with a stream passing through it. Cross the stream via the stone footbridge, bearing left (SE) to a stile into woodland; here find granite boulders covered in mosses and a woodland floor inhabited by bluebells, wood sorrel and violets in season.

Take the left fork to Lovaton. After a second stile look for a further stile in the hedge on the right and exit onto a minor road. Turn left along the road to Lovaton. At the telephone kiosk bear left and climb.

Where the road bears right take the path indicated on the left to Marchant's Cross (¼ m). Pass through two gates and follow the grassy path to another gate into a field. Walk diagonally across this field, which has a standing stone in the centre. Pass into a second field and follow a Northerly course to descend to a stile in the far right corner. Once onto the road turn left to descend to the 600 year old, 8 feet high Marchant's Cross, the tallest of Dartmoor's crosses. There is a cross carved on each face and legend says that wayfarers about to cross the moor would pray here that they might not encounter danger on their journey.

Turn right along the lane to Sheepstor and continue to Yeo Farm. At Yeo Farm take a few minutes to study the partially ruined farmhouse, built in 1610. Over the door are the initials I.W., thought to be those of a former owner, John or Iohn Wood.

The path turns right (NE), just prior to the old farmhouse, over a wall and stile to woodland ahead; the path is waymarked. Turn left as the woodland is entered and climb a stile to follow a grassy path which rises above the farmhouse and rejoins the farm track. There are views over Meavy from here.

Bear left between stone walls and follow the waymarking to a ladder stile into Burrator Wood. In Springtime this is a wonderful sight - the floor of the wood is a carpet of bluebells and the scent is quite heady. Leave the wood via a gap in the wall; over a stile and follow the path to a stone step stile over a wall into a field. Once into this field the massive granite bulk of Sheepstor is straight ahead. Keep to the left hand edge of the field, pass through the gate on the left and enter the field to the right. Bear NE to descend to a track; follow the track to a wooden gate onto the road.

Turn left along the road to Sheepstor village. At the T-junction go straight across into St. Leonard's church. On entering the porch look up to see the sundial (dating from 1640) over it in the form of a skull with corn growing from it - this symbolises life after death. The initials J.E. refer to John Elford, Lord of the Manor of nearby Longstone during the 17th century. All that remains of the manor house is the porch and hall, still recognisable on the shore of Burrator reservoir. The church contains a 15th century font and there is fine carving on the ends of the pews depicting St. George slaying the dragon, a shepherd, a cockerel with a sheaf of corn, the signing of the Magna Carta and a bishop preaching to a king and queen. Also contained in the church is the story of the *'White*

St. Leonard's - Sheepstor.

Rajahs' of Sarawak.

Leaving the church porch turn left to continue through the churchyard, passing the tombs of Sir James and Sir Charles Brooke, to two metal gates leading onto the road. Bear left along the road to the junction at Lambs Park, turning left uphill to arrive at the base of Sheepstor.

Climb the steep grassy hill through the granite clitter to pass Pixies' Cave, where it is said Squire Elford hid from Cromwell's troops. Over the years the rocks have moved forward and the cave now appears as a dark cleft close to the ground. Once atop this massive tor take in the tremendous views over the surrounding countryside. At the East end of the tor, on the summit, discover the rocks known as the *'Feather Bed'*.

Leave the tor, taking a NNW course towards the plantation and stone wall below. Follow the wall down to the left hand corner of the plantation, to a gate onto a track between walls.

Follow the track to the road, turning left and then right at the T-junction. Continue along the road beside reservoir, or take the footpath running alongside the reservoir, exiting onto the road again before the dam. At the dam turn right.

★　　　　　　　★　　　　　　　★

MARY TAVY - HORNDON

VIA PETER TAVY

Distance:	Approx. 5 miles
Time:	Allow 3 - 4 hours
Map:	Landranger 191; Outdoor Leisure 28; Pathfinder SX47/57 & SX48/58
Start reference:	SX509787
Terrain:	Rough tracks, field paths, some roads, muddy
Nearest Town:	Tavistock
Parking:	Mary Tavy Church
Refreshments:	Elephant's Nest Inn, Horndon
Church:	St. Mary, Mary Tavy
Connection:	William Crossing (1847 -1928) Author

William Crossing wrote regular articles for local newspapers, including the Western Morning News. Two of these series, 'A Hundred Years on Dartmoor' and 'Gems in a Granite Setting' were later published in book form. However, his masterpiece is his 'Guide to Dartmoor', which was first published in 1909. As well as his Dartmoor works, he also wrote poetry and plays.

He lived for many years in a cottage, now called 'Crossings', at Mary Tavy. There is a memorial tablet affixed to the cottage, which was unveiled in 1952, informing the reader that this is where the 'Guide to Dartmoor' was written.

From the church continue along the lane (South) and shortly the metalled road becomes a rough track passing a footpath sign to Peter Tavy (½ m). Through a gate bear left over the bridge crossing the River Tavy and turn right onto the bridlepath to Peter Tavy. The track climbs and shortly the tower of Peter Tavy church is seen; bear left at a junction in the path to pass St. Peter's Church. Follow the lane to its junction with the road.

At the junction turn right continuing down the road to a turning on the left. Turn left by the Post Office and immediately bear left onto the bridleway to Combe. After a short distance the path emerges onto a metalled road.

Turn left over the bridge and climb, passing Combe Cottages. This lane is bordered by boulders on which grows dogs tooth lichen. The road shortly becomes a narrow path and through a gate the way divides. Take the path indicated to Lower Godsworthy, to ascend through bracken and gorse to a stone wall with a waymarked post. Climb the wall into a rough field just below Smeardon Down.

Take an Easterly course across this field to a gate in a wall; follow the wide grassy path to a metalled lane. At the lane turn left and continue until a sign is reached on the right indicating to Stephen's Grave and White Tor. There are wonderful views across the moorland from this track. Take the stony track leading to White Tor and climb once again. Look out for skylarks in the bracken on the moor.

The track levels and Boulters Tor is passed (left). There are more splendid views across Dartmoor from here. Immediately after Boulters Tor a wall commences on the left. Locate a line of stones beside a grassy path on the left and turn onto this path, leading North between the line of stones (left) and the wall. At the gate into the field the path is signposted.

Keeping the wall to the left descend through the field, passing through a small gate into a second field. Continue descending until the path bears right to cross a small bridge over a stream, thence rejoining a metalled lane; turn left along the lane.

Arriving at the minor road at Cudlipptown, turn right and climb. After about a mile take the footpath indicated on the left which leads through a rough field. Keep to the right of the field and descend through docks, thistles and sorrel, to take the narrow path leading Eastwards alongside the river. At the waymarker post descend to the river and Horndon Bridge, bearing left over

St. Mary - Mary Tavy

the bridge to climb the stony track ahead, arriving at Horndon.

It is believed Horndon became a settlement arising out of miners' huts which were sited here during the days when there were many flourishing mines in the area. Lead, silver, arsenic and tin were extracted and the area even produced its own coinage.

Pass through the hamlet of Horndon and take the left fork to arrive at the minor road to Mary Tavy. Turn left along the road for a short distance to reach the Elephant's Nest Inn (left), containing many elephant pictures and ornaments. On leaving the Inn continue along the road for about 500 yards, then take the unmade track on the left. Follow this track to a path through fields.

Keep to the right hand side of the first two fields, then bear left through a third field to a stone step stile over a wall. Over the stile, keep a SSW course through the next field to join a grassy path (signposted) as it descends towards the remains of old mine workings, where the chimney still stands.

The path continues over a ladder stile and descends beside a field. At the bottom of the field turn left and walk to the far corner of the field then pass through the gate on the right. The tower of Mary Tavy church is ahead. Walk towards the church and a stone step stile over the wall leads into the churchyard.

It is at the top of this churchyard that William Crossing and his wife Emma lie, under the shade of a sycamore tree. Standing by the grave one can see the Western slopes of the Dartmoor Crossing loved. The footpath descends to the right of the church.

The Church of St. Mary was built mainly during the reign of Henry VI. On entering the church notice the sundial over the porch and the ancient stocks within. The church was much restored in 1879 and the screen, though medieval in style, is 19th century, as are the stained glass windows.

LEWTRENCHARD

Distance:	Approx. 2½ miles
Time:	Allow 1 - 2 hours
Map:	OS Landranger 201; Pathfinder SX48/58
Start reference:	SX457862
Terrain:	Roads and paths; wet in places; wade through River Lew (usually ankle deep)
Nearest Town:	Tavistock
Parking:	Near church
Church:	St. Peter's, Lewtrenchard
Connection:	Sabine Baring-Gould (1834-1924) Author, hymn & carol writer

Lewtrenchard was home to Sabine Baring-Gould for over 40 years. His best know hymn is *'Onward Christian Soldiers'* but he also wrote the carols *'The Infant King'*, *'Gabriel's Message'* and *'Sleep my Saviour Sleep'*; he was the author of many books, novels and short stories. The Manor was built in 1620 and has belonged to the Baring-Gould family since 1626. Sabine Baring-Gould inherited the estate on the death of his father in 1872, but did not become Rector until 1881, following the death of his uncle. The Manor is now run as a Country House Hotel and Restaurant, still housing many of the original paintings and furnishings accumulated by Sabine Baring-Gould. The links between church and Manor are maintained at Harvest Thanksgiving when a Harvest Supper is held at the Manor for the parishioners.

From the church walk along the road in an Easterly direction passing Lewtrenchard Manor on the right. Notice the curiously shaped dovecot in the Manor grounds and after a short distance, having passed the main building of the Manor, a tree lined walk will be seen leading from the garden and running parallel with the road. This path is known as *'Madam's Walk'* - a reference to Margaret Belfield Gould (died 1795), who worked extremely hard to save Lewtrenchard Manor; it is rumoured that she walks the house and grounds on occasions.

Lewtrenchard Manor.

Continue along this road lined by sycamore, beech, elder and chestnut trees. There are a number of mosses clinging to the stone walls enclosing the Manor grounds as well as hart's tongue and maidenhair spleenwort ferns enjoying the dampness here. In Autumn, horse mushrooms may be found growing around the bases of the tree trunks. Concealed within this woodland are huge mounds of stones and slate left over from the heyday of the local quarry, now covered by ferns, nettles and brambles.

The road opens up to a view of the surrounding hills and woodland - away to the right is Eastcottdown plantation and Lew Wood. A glance back reveals further evidence of the past quarrying, which provided the stone and slate for the building of the Manor. Walking on beneath ancient oak trees, a turning on the right is reached, indicating Lew Mill. Turn here passing between a number of lime trees, and Lew Mill will shortly come into sight. On rounding the bend, there is the Dower House, built in 1664, with a 16 foot menhir (a Bronze Age single standing stone) standing twixt Mill and House.

Shortly after the Mill and its farm buildings are left behind a bridge is reached over the River Lew. Just after crossing the bridge a public footpath sign is reached and here there is a choice of route; follow the path SSW across the field, which could be very wet, or continue on along the road between low hedges containing holly, hazel and bracken, until a T-junction is reached. From this road there are some wonderful views across the countryside, making it difficult to accept that the busy A30 is only a stone's throw away.

At the T-junction, turn right along a metalled track indicated as a 'No through road'; a gradual climb with wonderful views opening up on the right. It is possible to look back to the Mill and Dower House and the old quarry is easily discernible, topped by trees; shortly the footpath through the field exits onto this track.

This metalled track ceases as it enters Wooda Farm yard. Keeping the outbuildings to the left pass the left-hand side of the farmhouse and walk up a track, which rises fairly steeply. When the track levels there is a branching of the ways. To the left is a wooden gate onto a track leading upwards beneath trees, but take the right hand track which descends. There are trees lining the way and the banks are covered with mosses and ferns, including the hard fern with its comb-like fronds.

The descent becomes more gradual and a point is reached where another choice of route awaits. To the right is a signposted footpath leading NNW across a filed which will emerge onto a track just prior to the river; alternatively continue along the original route to a T-junction, where Lew and Raddon Forestry Estates are indicated on the left. Turn right along this wide track and after a short distance the River Lew is reached. Wade through the river and continue following the wide track, overhung by beech and sycamore trees.

St. Peter - Lewtrenchard

Shortly the picturesque quarry cottages are reached and the track returns to a metalled road. Once again there are lovely views away to the left. Bear right at the junction with the minor road and on passing alongside a stone barn notice the 'V.R.' post box in the wall.

Ahead is the turning for Lewtrenchard Manor and the church and on the corner is a memorial seat to Michael Baring-Gould (1937 - 1986), a great-grandson of Sabine.

Walk on to the church of St. Peter, which contains so much of interest. There are lime trees forming an avenue to the entrance porch and just prior to the porch, on the right hand side, is the Baring-Gould family vault; however, Sabine and his wife Grace are buried in the shadow of the tower. Inspect the outside of the church tower and discover the stone ledgers affixed to the walls.

On entering this cosy church, the most impressive sight is the large Rood Screen, which is, as far as possible, a copy of the original 16th century screen. The carved bench ends are very varied in the detail they depict, some have initials on, some coats-of-arms, whilst others show tools such as those used by a farrier. These and the rest of the beautifully preserved interior of the church is largely due to Sabine Baring-Gould, who was a collector of anything interesting.

There are stone ledgers and beautifully polished brass plaques in memory of the many members of the Baring-Gould family. The 15th century triptych (three hinged panels with pictures) was presented to the church in 1881 by a Colchester lady. Sabine Baring-Gould was Rector at East Mersea, on Mersea Island, some ten miles from Colchester from 1871 - 1881. Could this lady have known of his 'magpie' habits and decided this beautiful painting would be safer in his keeping?

★   ★   ★

MOLLAND - BREMLEY
VIA SMALLACOMBE & GOURTE

Distance:	Approx. 3.5 miles
Time:	Allow 3 hours
Map:	OS Landranger 181 Pathfinder SS82/92
Start reference:	SS806284
Terrain:	Arduous - rough tracks, moorland & field paths; wet and muddy in places; several steep climbs
Nearest Town:	South Moulton
Parking:	Area below church in Molland
Refreshments:	London Inn, Molland
Church:	St. Mary, Molland
Connection:	Reverend John Froude (1777 - 1852)*

Legendary character *'Wicked Parson Froude'*'

This small village on the edge of Exmoor has a beautiful church with an interesting history. The legendary figure of the Reverend John Froude, who was the incumbent at nearby Knowstone, also preached here. Many stories surround this rather lawless character , whom it was said organised bands of thugs to burn, or otherwise destroy, the property of anyone who offended him. It is not surprising that he became known as *'Wicked Parson Froude'*. He died in a fit of rage, being unable to revenge a young farmer who had removed a shrub growing in front of his parlour window. He was the character upon whom R.D.Blackmore based 'Parson Chowne' in his novel *The Maid of Sker* (1872).

From the parking area take an Easterly course away from the church and walk along the narrow road, passing the Vicarage on the left. The road passes between high banks of hazel, beech and sycamore, lined with bluebells and primroses in Spring, and climbs gradually to a sharp left hand bend. Follow the road to Sandyway, Hawkbridge and Withypool as it climbs steeply now. Just before the crest of the hill is reached look for a metal gateway on the right, with a small wooden gate in the bank on the opposite side of the road. There is a public footpath sign here, although it may be obscured by the hedge.

Once over the metal gate follow the track across the field, walking in a NNE direction. The track drops onto a lower level; keeping the same course descend to a narrow overgrown path beside a small stream on the right. A wooden stile is reached where there is water to be negotiated on both sides of the stile.

From the stile climb up the side of the field keeping the hedge-row to the left, continuing in a NNE direction. As you climb look around at the view beginning to open up; Exmoor is to the left and away to the right is the Yeo Valley. As the way levels look to the right-hand corner of the field to see a gateway leading out onto a metalled track. Cross over this track and walk down that leading to Smallacombe, ignoring the unmade track to the left.

Descend the track to Smallacombe between hedges of hazel, oak and sycamore, made colourful by rosebay-willowherb, fox-gloves and tormentil in season. At the end of this track is a wooden gate, another stream and very probably a considerable amount of mud! This is the start of the moorland and there are many sheep grazing here, so be sure to shut the gate behind you.

Keep a course ENE through the gorse and bracken as the way climbs uphill onto the moor. Take time to look around - the colours of the moorland are beautiful with many different shades of green and in Autumn the golds and browns of the deciduous trees.

The gorse and bracken close in and there are clumps of heather, and many hawthorn trees with their attractive red berries in Autumn. A large beech tree is passed on the right and shortly another stream is forded by means of stepping stones. Another steep climb and an open view of Molland Common is gained. Continue along this stony path to descend into a small area of woodland. Ahead is another stream from where the path turns right and ascends beside a stone wall beneath overhanging trees. The way is very rough and stony with a view gradually opening up on the right. Go quietly along this part of the route as there is a possibility of spotting some red deer, sharing the grazing with the sheep and cows.

Where the path emerges from the overhanging trees there is a gate on the right with *'Brimblecombe'* and *'Please Shut Gate'* marked on it . Go through this gateway and follow the rough track, now heading South, as it descends between fields. A large coniferous wood stands on the other side of the valley, there are open views across fields to the left and back up to Molland Common with the Yeo Valley away to the right.

When this track ends at a T-junction, turn right and continue descending a stony track beneath an avenue of hawthorn and rowan trees. Here the banks are covered in moss and delicate ferns delight in the cool damp shade. Pass through a gateway and, with a property on the left, turn right bearing SW along a narrow path beneath trees bordered by fields on both sides. Here the path is well distinguished but very uneven and stony and may be muddy after wet weather.

The path enters woodland and twists and turns as it goes. This is mixed deciduous woodland, with rhododendrons providing a splash of colour in the Spring.

Keeping the small stream to your left continue walking in a generally SW direction until a point is reached where the stream can be crossed and a steep climb is made up the opposite bank to join a wide dirt track through a coniferous plantation. Follow the track as it emerges via a gateway into a large field, where yet more sheep may be encountered. Again there are marvellous open views from this point.

The track continues its descent and when the buildings of Gourte Farm are reached, bear left onto the now metalled track leading away from the farm. Ascend to a junction of minor roads and tracks at Bremley Cross; from this point take the narrow road signposted to Molland.

This road descends between high hedges and leads to a small bridge over a tributary to the River Yeo. At this point the road bends sharp left and with a cottage just in view, look for the signposted footpath to the right, climbing steeply through a field. Having scrambled to the top of the ridge turn around and once again take in the beautiful scenery.

From this point the way ahead is due West. Take the route over the five-bar stile and keep to the top of the field with the hedgerow on the right. Through a gateway into another field, continue along by the hedgerow and over a small wooden gate into a third field from where the tower of Molland Church may be glimpsed. In the right hand corner of this field is another stile leading onto a narrow road to Molland.

The road descends and then climbs steeply again before rounding a bend and levelling out alongside the Methodist Chapel. From here it is only a short distance to the village.

Enter the 15th century church of St. Mary Magdalene, parts of which date back to the Norman era. Immediately upon setting foot inside you are dwarfed by the tall box pews. Straight ahead are four arches linking the North aisle to the nave - notice the precarious angle at which they lean, although they are apparently safe. Another striking feature is the three-decker pulpit with sounding board over. The altar is dominated by a large memorial to the Reverend Daniel Berry and adjacent is a smaller memorial to the Courtenay family with, below, a heart-box surrounded by iron railings thought to contain the hearts of a Courtenay and his wife.

* see Knowstone walk

★   ★   ★

St. Mary Magdalene - Molland

KNOWSTONE - MILLHAVEN
VIA LUCKETT

Distance:	Approx. 2½ miles
Time:	Allow 2 hours
Map:	OS Landranger 181 Pathfinder SS82/92
Start reference:	SS829231
Terrain:	Fields & woodland paths; some minor roads
Nearest Town:	South Molton
Parking:	Beside church in Knowstone
Refreshments:	Mason Arms, Knowstone
Church:	St. Peter, Knowstone
Connection	Reverend John Froude (1777 - 1852)*
Legendary character	*'Wicked Parson Froude'*
	Sir Nicholas Wadham (Died 1610)**
	Founder of Wadham College, Oxford

The Legendary figure of the Reverend John Froude was the incumbent here for almost half a century. It is said that his ghost walks the lanes at night.

Sir Nicholas Wadham lived at the house of the same name, situated on the road to Molland. Today, it is a farmhouse dating from the 18th century.

Take the pathway into the churchyard and enter the church via the Norman door. The chancel hides an interesting feature; move the curtains covering the wall behind the altar and discover the Ten Commandments and the Apostles Creed painted there. A large memorial to the Froude family is on the North wall of the chancel. Leaving the church, exit via the gates at the top of the churchyard.

Pass the old school and once more rejoin the road, turning left in front of a row of cottages. Continue to the last cottage in this

St. Peter - Knowstone

row and take the signposted footpath on the right, through a small gate. Keep straight ahead to a stile and enter a field. Bear slightly right (North) across this field to a gate, bearing a yellow waymarking arrow. Over the gate, cross the next field to another gate with a further waymarking arrow.

Take a Northerly course across this field, descending towards the woodland and the Crooked Oak river. Bear left through a gate and follow alongside the river, which is lined by oak, birch and hazel, with mixed woodland on the far side. In Autumn the trees provide a myriad of colours from many shades of green through to gold and russet.

Continue beside the river, passing through farm buildings. Exit via a gate onto a minor road. To the right is Luckett, the bridge over the Crooked Oak, with the road leading onto Wadham; but turn left here and immediately start climbing.

The road is tree-lined, giving dappled shade, and the banks are home to many mosses and ferns, including the hard fern; primroses and foxgloves may also be found. At the top of the hill, turn right along the road to Ash Mill.

Follow this quiet lane for about a mile to a public footpath indicated on the left. Take the path through the garden of Millhaven and upwards into woodland. Here again are oaks, hazel and holly, making a splendid show in the Autumn. Take an Easterly course through the trees to emerge at a gate into a large field.

Continue the Easterly course through the field to a stile leading onto a road to Knowstone. Bear right along the road for a short distance then take the footpath on the left, just after the Knowstone village sign.

On entering the field, there is a wonderful view across the village with the church tower rising above all. Walk through the field toward the church, locating the stile at the far end to exit into a track. Turn right and then left along the road to return to the church.

* See Molland walk
** See Branscombe walk